THE CAUSES
OF THE
COLD WAR

STEWART ROSS

WORLD ALMANAC® LIBRARY

Please visit our web site at: www.worldalmanaclibrary.com
For a free color catalog describing World Almanac® Library's
list of high-quality books and multimedia programs,
call 1-800-848-2928 or fax your request to (414) 332-3567.

Library of Congress Cataloging-in-Publication Data

Ross, Stewart.
    The causes of the Cold War / by Stewart Ross.
      p. cm. — (The Cold War)
    Includes bibliographical references and index.
    Summary: Explores the rivalry and tensions between the United States and the Soviet Union stemming
from their differing ideologies and discusses the resulting events during the decade after World War II.
    ISBN 0-8368-5272-9 (lib. bdg.)
    ISBN 0-8368-5277-X (softcover)
    1. Cold war—Juvenile literature. 2. World politics—1945—Juvenile literature. 3. United States—Foreign
relations—Soviet Union—Juvenile literature. 4. Soviet Union—Foreign relations—United States—Juvenile literature.
[1. Cold war. 2. World politics—1945-. 3. United States—Foreign relations—Soviet Union. 4. Soviet Union—
Foreign relations—United States.] I. Title. II. Series.
D843.G6548   2002
327.73047—dc21   2001046604

This North American edition first published in 2002 by
World Almanac® Library
330 West Olive Street, Suite 100
Milwaukee, WI 53212 USA

This U.S. edition © 2002 by World Almanac® Library. Original edition published in Great Britain
in 2001 by Hodder Wayland, a division of Hodder Children's Books. Additional end matter
© 2002 by World Almanac® Library.

Series concept: Alex Woolf
Editor: Nicola Edwards
Designer: Derek Lee
Consultant: Scott Lucas, Head of American and Canadian Studies, University of Birmingham
Proofreader: Sue Lightfoot
Map illustrator: Nick Hawken
World Almanac® Library designer: Scott M. Krall
World Almanac® Library editor: Jim Mezzanotte
World Almanac® Library production: Susan Ashley and Jessica L. Yanke

Picture credits: AKG photo: cover (left), 6, 12, 23, 25, 36, 37, 38, 42, 53, 54, 59; Camera Press: 50; Corbis:
cover (center), title page, 43; HWPL: 8, 14 © National Maritime Museum, 15 © Imperial War Museum, 18,
19, 24 © Imperial War Museum, 31 © Associated Press, 44, 45, 60 (both), 61 (top) © Imperial War Museum,
61 (bottom); Peter Newark: cover (right), 5, 7, 9, 13, 16, 17, 20, 22, 39, 48, 52, 55, 56, 58; Popperfoto: 4, 10,
11, 27, 28, 30, 33, 34, 35, 41, 47, 49, 51, 57; Topham: 26, 29, 32

All rights reserved. No part of this book may be reproduced, stored in a retrieval system, or transmitted in any
form or by any means, electronic, mechanical, photocopying, recording, or otherwise without the prior written
permission of the copyright holder.

Printed in the United States of America

1 2 3 4 5 6 7 8 9 06 05 04 03 02

Contents

CHAPTER ONE

An Age Defined

A MEETING OF ALLIES

On the morning of April 25, 1945, less than two weeks before the end of World War II in Europe, patrols from the Sixty-ninth Division of the U.S. Army reached the western bank of the Elbe River in Germany. On the opposite bank they spotted Red Army soldiers from the Soviet Union, the United States' most powerful partner in the Allied forces.

Signaling that they were friends, the Americans crossed the river and were greeted by the Soviets with smiles and hugs. Vodka appeared, toasts were drunk, someone produced an accordion, and before long, an impromptu party was in full swing to celebrate the first meeting of these Allied front lines.

▼ A carefully posed photograph of the first meeting of U.S. and Soviet troops on April 25, 1945. The apparent warmth of this greeting was soon frozen by the coming of the Cold War.

AN IRON CURTAIN

The young men and women (many females served in the Red Army) reportedly swore vague oaths of comradeship, but they were prevented by language barriers from holding any meaningful conversations — a situation that would have significant implications. Like their soldiers, the U.S. and Soviet governments expressed friendship but spoke and thought in very different languages. The Americans came from the world of liberal democracy, the Russians from the world of communism. The two worlds were not compatible.

Only weeks after the soldiers met, British prime minister Winston Churchill used a phrase he was later to make famous. He was worried, he wrote to U.S. president Harry Truman, that the Red Army had drawn an "iron curtain" across Europe. There were no more toasts and dancing. Instead, the United States and the Soviet Union, each allied with other countries, began drifting farther apart, and by 1948 they stood at the very brink of war. Outright war never occurred, but the two countries did engage in four decades of an open, dangerous rivalry known as the Cold War.

THE ARMS RACE

In 1947, U.S. presidential advisor Bernard Baruch first used the phrase "Cold War" to describe the struggle between the U.S.-led "Western" bloc of countries and the Soviet-led "Eastern" bloc. Unlike a conventional war, or "hot war," this struggle did not usually involve the actual use of weapons, but it did involve each side building up weapons to outstrip the other side's military power. This "arms race" became the Cold War's most prominent feature.

EAST AND WEST

The depth of East-West mistrust is clearly shown in these two extracts, both from 1946. The first was written by George Kennan, a U.S. diplomat working in Moscow, and the second by Nikolai Novikov, the Soviet ambassador stationed in Washington, D.C.

" ... we have here a political force [the USSR] committed fanatically to the belief that with the U.S. there can be no permanent modus vivendi [working together], that it is desirable and necessary that the internal harmony of our society be disrupted, our traditional way of life be destroyed, the international authority of our state be broken."

"The foreign policy of the United States, which reflects the imperialist tendencies of American monopolistic capital, is characterized in the postwar period by a striving for world supremacy."

▼ The sign in this French anti-Soviet cartoon of 1935 reads "We are very happy." Before 1941, hostility towards the communists was widespread in the Western press.

5

▲ The Apollo 11 Moon landing in 1969 showed that the United States had taken a firm lead in its space race with the Soviet Union, after falling behind in the 1950s.

A DIVIDED WORLD

The United States and the Soviet Union were not alone in their struggle. Several other nations — for example, Britain, France, Italy, China, and Czechoslovakia — played a significant role in the Cold War's development.

As the Cold War deepened, each side sought allies. After swallowing up much of Eastern Europe, the Soviets went looking elsewhere to support communist regimes. The United States, meanwhile, strengthened its ties with Britain and Western Europe and built up new friendships in Latin America, Australia, and Asia. The communist takeover in China in 1949 added a new, unpredictable dimension to Cold War tensions (see page 45).

East-West rivalry also influenced lesser confrontations and conflicts. For instance, it helped shape the Arab-Israeli wars and the breakup of European empires in Africa and elsewhere. In Europe, this rivalry played a key factor in the development of what is now the European Union.

A NEAR-TOTAL CONFLICT

Although the Cold War primarily involved an arms race and diplomatic confrontations between the United States and the Soviet Union, the two sides also used other strategies against

6

each other, including economic pressure (see pages 22–23) and both official and unofficial propaganda (see page 56). All of these strategies made the Cold War almost as "total" a war as World War II. The Cold War distorted (and finally destroyed) the Soviet economy by diverting a huge amount of national wealth to military needs. Military demands on both sides also spurred rapid technological development, notably in aviation and communications. The Cold War produced a "space race" that brought about orbital satellites and the first moon landing in 1969.

A nuclear standoff between the United States and the Soviet Union spawned films, novels, poetry, and a brand new genre of spy thrillers, and it also produced paranoia and jingoism. Even athletes were encouraged to be ambassadors for a whole way of life.

STABILITY THROUGH FEAR

It can be argued that the Cold War actually brought a stability to the world that had been missing since 1914. Two major power blocs simplified international politics. As much by luck as by good judgement, the Cold War did not bring about a global nuclear catastrophe. Not many would have predicted such an outcome in the dark years following World War II.

SOVIET SYSTEM IS BEST

There was great admiration for the way the Red Army had defeated Nazi troops in the East. In 1946, Joseph Stalin, the Soviet leader, claimed that this defeat proved the superiority of what he called the "Soviet social system":

"The war has shown that the Soviet social system is a ... perfectly viable and stable form of organization of society. More than that, ... the Soviet social system has proved more viable and stable than a non-Soviet social system ... [and] a better form of organization of society."

▶ Soviet leader Joseph Dzhugashvili, more commonly known as "Stalin" (Russian for "man of steel"), was determined to defend the interests of his country against encircling capitalism.

The Roots of the Cold War

A CONFLICT OF IDEOLOGY

Unlike conventional wars, the Cold War did not follow a declaration of war or a sudden act of aggression. The Cold War brought about its changes slowly, until, by 1950, it dominated international politics. Its roots lay deep in the past.

The Cold War was essentially a conflict between two ideologies and their respective systems of government. Liberal democracy, an ideology embraced by the United States, Britain, and other Western countries, advocates rule by elected representatives and holds that a government might broadly regulate a capitalist, or free market, economy but should not otherwise attempt to control it. Communism, as embraced by the Soviets and later by China, is an ideology that advocates authoritarian rule by a single party and holds that a government should own all businesses and control the economy.

▼ Karl Marx, the German philosopher who foretold the eventual collapse of capitalism while in exile in Britain, the cradle of the capitalist system.

KARL MARX

Modern communism is the brainchild of the German philosopher Karl Marx (1818–1883). Marx believed that history, like science, operates by knowable laws. According to these laws, a society moves through three stages of development: feudalism, capitalism, and finally communism. Economic change, Marx believed, was the engine that would move a society through these stages.

Marx argued that the capitalist, free-market way of life was doomed. A society's available wealth would find its way into the hands of fewer and fewer business owners, or

8

"capitalists," who would try to gain profits by paying less wages to the working class, or "proletariat." Eventually, Marx argued, the proletariat would grow tired of being exploited. They would overthrow the capitalists and establish a classless society in which there was no private property and everyone was treated equally.

REVOLUTION

Marx believed that a temporary government, which he called the "dictatorship of the proletariat," would be needed after the fall of capitalism. This government would be led by a band of communists dedicated to weeding out the last remnants of capitalism and class-based thinking.

Marx's theories were first put to the test not in a major industrial country, such as the United States or Britain, but in Russia, a largely agricultural and old-fashioned empire. The Bolsheviks, a group of communists led by Vladimir Lenin, seized power in Russia in 1917. After defeating all their opponents in a bloody civil war (1918–1921), they proceeded to establish the world's first communist state.

VLADIMIR LENIN (1870–1924)

Born Vladimir Ilyich Ulyanov, Lenin was first inspired by the works of Karl Marx at the age of nineteen. Lenin's most important contribution to Marxist thought was his belief that a society such as Russia's could pass from feudalism to communism without going through the capitalist stage of development. After seizing power in the Russian revolution of 1917, he attempted to put his ideas into practice. The result was the Soviet Union's communist system of government, which lasted for over seventy years.

▶ The dawn of a brave new world? A Soviet propaganda painting showing Lenin (with tie) amid a crowd of enthusiastic workers in 1917.

Guilty or not? A Soviet committee engaged in "purging" suspected dissidents from the Communist Party in 1933. By 1939, thousands of supposed enemies of Stalin's regime had been executed or imprisoned in inhumane labor camps.

DICTATORSHIP

One of communism's chief weaknesses appeared the moment Lenin seized power: how were the new leaders to be kept in check? Lenin genuinely wished to help ordinary Russians by giving them decent wages, education, and health care, but many of his followers were more interested in advancing their own careers. In addition, Lenin's belief in the righteousness of his cause led him to establish a one-party state in which no opposition was tolerated.

Any hope that the new Soviet Union might develop into a communist utopia was ended in 1928, when Joseph Stalin came to power. A ruthless and paranoid dictator, Stalin ruled the Soviet Union through the Communist Party until his death in 1953. Until 1941, he enforced five-year modernization plans for Soviet industry. At the same time, he sanctioned the slaughter of millions of innocent peasants and purged the party, the government, and the armed forces of anyone he suspected of opposing him. The full extent of his crimes did not come to light until after the collapse of the Soviet Union in 1991.

RUSSIA AND THE WEST

In 1917, the Bolsheviks overthrew a provisional government that endorsed the principles of liberal democracy. This act turned Western governments against the Bolsheviks from the start. During the Russian Civil War that followed, Britain and several other Western governments sent troops to support the "White" opponents of the "Red" communists.

Western-style democracies remained suspicious of the one-party Bolshevik state throughout the 1920s and 1930s, and the Soviets increased this suspicion by supporting revolutionary communist parties in other countries. The United States did not formally recognize the Union of Soviet Socialist Republics (USSR) until 1933, eleven years after its formation.

UNLIKELY ALLIES

Hostility between the Soviet Union and Western governments continued until World War II. At that time, the hostility did not so much end as cool off, because of the practical necessity of defeating a common enemy: Nazi Germany.

In August 1939, Germany and the Soviet Union shocked Western leaders by signing a non-aggression pact. Hitler had bitterly opposed communism, but by signing this pact he did not have to worry about the Soviets and could concentrate on attacking Western Europe. After Nazi victories in France and the Low Countries in June 1941, however, Hitler launched a massive assault on the Soviet Union. For the next four years, the Soviets and the Western liberal democracies had no choice but to fight together.

JOSEPH STALIN (1879–1953)

Stalin joined the Bolshevik party long before the 1917 revolution. After Lenin's death in 1924, he used his position as party secretary to isolate and eliminate his rivals. As head of the Soviet state, he modernized the country and led it to victory over the Nazis. He did so, however, at the cost of millions of lives. Modern Russia still bears the scars of his dictatorship, which was arguably the most brutal of modern times.

▼ The pact that shocked the world: Molotov, the Soviet commissar for foreign affairs, signs the Nazi-Soviet Pact in August 1939.

LIBERAL DEMOCRACY

The roots of liberal democracy stretch back to the English Revolution in the seventeenth century. After this revolution, England's representative parliament, rather than the country's monarch, became the key component of the English political system. In the next century, the English Revolution and new ideas about government inspired revolutions in the American colonies and in France. These two upheavals further developed the principles of liberal democracy.

In a modern liberal democracy, no individual, group, or institution has supreme power. If there is a monarch — as is still the case in Britain — he or she has no authority. Ultimate power lies in the hands of the people, who elect their leaders. The elected government makes laws that apply to all citizens alike, including members of the government. Different political parties each offer their own ideas on the best way to govern. All individuals are free to express their own opinions, even if they disagree with the government's actions.

▼ People power. Citizens of Paris storm a royal fortress and prison called the Bastille at the start of the French Revolution in July 1789.

BY THE PEOPLE OR FOR THE PEOPLE?

Soviet leaders claimed to believe in democracy, which was described by U.S. president Abraham Lincoln as "government of the people, by the people, for the people." Western democracies, however, emphasized government by the people, whereas the Soviets sought government for the people.

These two interpretations each had important ramifications for the way people lived. In most Western democracies there was an emphasis on individual freedom and choice, but there was also a wide gap between the rich and the poor. In the Soviet Union, on the other hand, income levels were roughly the same for everyone, if mostly lower than in the West, and there was no unemployment. Soviet leaders, however, banned all criticism of the government, because such criticism was considered backward-looking and antisocial.

CAPITALISM VS. COMMUNISM

In the Soviet Union, the state owned all wealth, and a central bureaucracy set wages, rents, and prices. This system eliminated most poverty, but it also stifled initiative. Most Russians saw no point in hard work if the state was the beneficiary, particularly if, as so many believed, the Soviet government was corrupt.

The United States and other Western democracies followed a capitalist, or "free enterprise," system, in which competition in an open market decides prices and wages, and government only regulates the market to a slight degree. In this system, an individual's wealth depends on environment and circumstance as well as personal effort.

▼ In 1787, delegates to the Constitutional Convention, held in Philadelphia, Pennsylvania, sign the newly drafted Constitution. This document provided a template for liberal democracy around the world.

FREEDOM OF SPEECH

Freedom of speech is a key part of most Western democracies. This freedom was guaranteed to the American people in the first amendment to the Constitution, ratified in 1791:

"Congress shall make no law respecting an establishment of religion, or prohibiting the free exercise thereof; or abridging the freedom of speech, or of the press; or of the right of the people peaceably to assemble, and to petition the government for a redress of grievances."

13

Japanese aircraft devastate U.S. warships in Pearl Harbor on December 7, 1941. The attack caused the United States to enter World War II on the side of Britain and its allies.

THE ARSENAL OF DEMOCRACY

In 1941, when the Nazis invaded the Soviet Union, Britain was the only major Western democracy waging war against fascism. The fascist nations Germany and Italy had overwhelmed most of Europe, except for neutral Sweden, Switzerland, and Spain. The United States was also technically a neutral country, but since 1940 it had supported Britain with a "bridge of ships" across the Atlantic.

U.S. president Franklin D. Roosevelt wanted the United States to be the "arsenal of democracy." With the Lend-Lease Act of 1941, Congress empowered him to provide equipment and supplies to any nation whose defense was thought necessary for American security. After Japan's attack on the U.S. naval base at Pearl Harbor on December 7, 1941, and Germany's subsequent declaration of war on the United States, the Soviet Union became a U.S. ally. By 1945 the United States had provided roughly $11 billion in lend-lease aid to the Soviet Union. Military necessity had forced the United States to become the arsenal of communism as well as of liberal democracy.

AMERICA'S PROBLEM

By early 1942, the United States was in a difficult position. It was at war with the Axis powers of Germany, Italy, and Japan, which, by the Anti-Comintern Pacts of 1936 and 1937, had declared their deep hostility to communism. As the world's most powerful liberal democracy, the United States was also bitterly opposed to communism. Yet it was now allied with the world's leading communist state, the Soviet Union.

This situation was further complicated by events in China. From the mid-1920s to the mid-1930s, China had been ravaged by a civil war between the Chinese Communist Party

(CCP) and the U.S.-backed Guomindang, or Kuomintang (KMT). When war broke out between China and Japan in 1937, the CCP and the KMT formed the Chinese United Front to fight together against Japanese invaders. The Japanese attack on Pearl Harbor brought the United States into alliance with the partly communist Chinese United Front.

By the fall of 1943, the Soviet Red Army was driving the Nazis out of Russia, the Allies had cleared Axis forces from North Africa and had invaded Italy, and the Japanese were retreating in the Pacific. With eventual victory now likely, the Soviet Union and the Western democracies turned their attention to the shape of the postwar world. Not surprisingly, their respective visions were very different.

FRANKLIN D. ROOSEVELT (1882–1945)

Born into a wealthy New York family, Roosevelt trained as a lawyer before entering politics. He made a name for himself as a reforming Democrat and was elected president of the United States in 1932, on the promise that he would combat the Depression. Many of his measures were successful, and his radio "fireside chats" to the nation brought him immense popularity. He was reelected in 1936, again in 1940, and yet again in 1944 — testimony to his skills as a leader in both peace and war.

▼ British gunners during the battle of El Alamein in Egypt in the fall of 1942. Allied victory in this battle marked the turning of the tide against Axis forces in World War II.

CHAPTER THREE

Planning for Peace

▲ Charter partners. Roosevelt (front left) and Churchill (front right) with officers of the H.M.S. *Prince of Wales,* on which the two leaders signed the Atlantic Charter on August 14, 1941.

THE ATLANTIC CHARTER

In August 1941, British prime minister Winston Churchill and U.S. president Franklin D. Roosevelt met on board a warship off the coast of Newfoundland. Together they produced a blueprint for the postwar world known as the Atlantic Charter.

The charter set out eight principles, including the right of people to choose their own government, free trade between nations, no territory to be seized by the Allies after the war, and no territory to change hands without its inhabitants' consent. A new international organization (the future United Nations) was proposed but not included in the charter. The Soviet Union, reeling from the Nazi invasion, was one of several nations to express support for the charter.

THE BIG THREE

The "Big Three" Allied leaders (Roosevelt, Churchill, and Stalin) met together for the first time in Tehran, Iran, in late November 1943. Stalin persuaded Roosevelt and Churchill to allow the expansion of the Soviet Union into Polish territory after the war. Stalin's request suggested that his support for the Atlantic Charter was pragmatic rather than heartfelt.

Churchill showed similar political cynicism when he met Stalin in Moscow in October 1944. The prime minister agreed that Romania and Bulgaria would fall within a Soviet sphere of influence, while Hungary and Yugoslavia would be subject to joint influence. Poland's fate was left undecided.

YALTA

With the war in Europe ended, the Big Three met again in February 1945 in Yalta, a town in the Crimea. At Stalin's insistence, the leaders agreed that the permanent members of

◄ The "Big Three" leaders (from left to right) Churchill, Roosevelt, and Stalin gather at the Yalta Conference in February 1945. Roosevelt has been criticized for taking too soft a line towards Stalin at the conference.

the United Nations' Security Council would each have veto power over all decisions, and they also agreed to divide Germany and Austria into separate zones of occupation. In addition, Roosevelt and Churchill reluctantly agreed that the Soviets could collect $20 billion in war reparations from Germany.

Poland was left within the Soviet sphere of influence, even though Roosevelt and Churchill probably realized that Stalin would not honor his promise to let the Poles freely elect their government. Eager for Stalin's assistance in the war against Japan, Roosevelt and Churchill had been forced to accept that the Soviets would now dominate Eastern Europe. Although Roosevelt kept the mood at Yalta friendly, to some observers the front lines of the future Cold War were now clear.

WINSTON S. CHURCHILL (1874–1965)

After serving in the British army, Churchill made a name for himself as a journalist before entering politics in 1900. His roller-coaster political career, which included two changes of party affiliation and several cabinet positions, seemed over by the 1930s. After his warnings about the dangers of Nazism proved correct, however, he was elected prime minister of Britain in May 1940. Churchill immediately recognized the importance of good relations with the United States and made much of his personal friendship with U.S. president Franklin Roosevelt.

A NEW PRESIDENT

After Roosevelt's death in April 1945, Vice President Harry S. Truman became the next U.S. president. The change in leadership was significant. Roosevelt hoped to build a postwar world based on U.S.-Soviet cooperation, ideally through the United Nations. To this end he had deliberately distanced himself from Churchill so that Stalin would not feel isolated. This strategy may have been unrealistic in the long run, but it did keep U.S.-Soviet relations amicable.

Three things can be said about Harry Truman in relation to the start of the Cold War. First, he was woefully ignorant of foreign affairs. He had met privately with Roosevelt only twice since the 1944 presidential election. Second, Truman was a straightforward man, with little patience for details, who believed that if the Soviets (or anyone else) broke their word, they should pay a price. Lastly, for four years Truman held the ultimate military trump card: the atomic bomb.

POTSDAM

The final summit meeting of the Big Three, held in Potsdam, Germany, began on July 17, 1945. The United States had successfully tested the first atomic bomb the day before, but Truman kept the news from Stalin for several days. At first, the meeting was between Stalin, Truman, and Churchill, but following Churchill's defeat in the July election, his place was taken by the new British prime minister, Clement Atlee. This change had little impact on the talks. Britain was bankrupt and exhausted from the war, and could not challenge the new world order being created by the two "superpowers."

Since Germany had surrendered on May 9, Truman's primary objective at Potsdam was getting Stalin to guarantee that the Soviet Union would enter the war against Japan. Stalin did so, but the Soviets' help proved unnecessary. With the nuclear destruction of Hiroshima and Nagasaki on August 6 and 9 respectively, Japan surrendered.

▼ New man, new problems. U.S. president Harry Truman stands between Stalin and Churchill at the opening of the Potsdam Conference on July 17, 1945. Truman might be glancing confidently towards Stalin because he knows something that Stalin does not — the United States has successfully tested an atomic bomb.

While Truman achieved his primary objective at Potsdam, Stalin also achieved many of his objectives. The Big Three leaders agreed to divide Germany into zones of occupation from which the Soviet Union could take reparations. This agreement left most of eastern Germany in Soviet hands. The Soviets were also allowed to keep Romania, Bulgaria, and Hungary within their sphere of influence. The fates of Poland and Czechoslovakia were less certain, but the Soviet presence in both countries did not bode well for liberal democracy in those places.

NUCLEAR WEAPONS

Employing 120,000 people in the United States, the "Manhattan Project" took three years to develop the atomic bombs that destroyed Hiroshima and Nagasaki. Although the project was top secret, it was infiltrated by Soviet spies who enabled the Soviets to build an atomic bomb much quicker than the United States expected. The power of the hydrogen bomb, which the United States first exploded on November 1, 1952, was a thousand times greater than the atomic bomb and raised the nuclear stakes to horrifying new levels.

◀ An atomic mushroom cloud rises over Nagasaki, Japan, on August 9, 1945. The terrifying shadow of "the bomb" hung over the world for the next forty-five years of the Cold War.

THE POSTWAR WORLD

The Second World War completely changed the world order. In 1939, the major powers of the world were Britain and Germany and to a lesser extent France and Italy. The Soviet Union, weakened by Stalin's paranoia, was an isolated and inward-looking country, while Japan challenged European control in the Far East. The United States, still recovering from the Depression, remained uncommitted to international affairs.

By 1945, Germany, France, Italy, and Japan were in ruins. While Britain had not been invaded and had lost less than one percent of its population, it had gone into serious decline and was negotiating a further $3.75 billion loan from the United States. Into the vacuum created by the collapse of these former powers stepped the United States and the Soviet Union, both of which were learning to play major roles on the world stage.

▼ A production line of Douglas Dauntless dive-bombers in Long Beach, California, stretches as far as the eye can see.

THE SUPERPOWERS

Unlike other countries, the United States emerged from the war a stronger, more prosperous nation. Its economy doubled during the war, making it the world's greatest industrial power. In 1945 alone, the country manufactured almost 50,000 aircraft (compared to the Soviets' 21,000) and 1,500 warships (compared to the Soviets' 11). Allied victory had been made possible by U.S. money and by 11.5 million U.S. troops. The United States also possessed nuclear weapons.

The Soviet Union, by comparison, was in relatively bad shape after the war. The country had lost over 27 million lives, while over 32,000 factories, 71,000 towns and villages, and 100,000 farms had been destroyed. On the other hand, the Soviet Union did possess an army of over 20 million soldiers — the largest ever assembled — and its communist ideology had appeal in countries that had been impoverished by war. Soviet-backed communist parties flourished in Eastern Europe and communism had supporters in Italy, France, Greece, and other Western nations. Even the British had rejected Churchill's Conservative Party in favor of the socialist Labour Party.

Some Soviet advisors thought the country should build on its popularity and adopt a more friendly attitude towards the West. Stalin and his foreign minister, Molotov, however, were angered at the United States' immediate end of lend-lease and its refusal to make further loans. They also argued that Russia had been brutally attacked by the West in 1812, 1914, and 1941. They were determined it would never happen again. Security would not come through fickle friendship but by building a buffer zone of dependent, communist states. Thus the Communist bloc came into being.

During World War II, the Soviet Union, Poland, and Yugoslavia lost more than ten percent of their populations, while Germany, Austria, and Greece lost between five and ten percent. France, Czechoslovakia, Hungary, the Netherlands, and Romania lost between one and five percent. Only Britain, Bulgaria, Italy, and Belgium had less than one percent population loss.

COUNTRY	MILITARY DEAD	CIVILIAN DEAD
SOVIET UNION	14.5 MILLION (M)	13 M
POLAND	850,000	5.8 M
YUGOSLAVIA	1.7 M (MILITARY AND CIVILIAN)	
GERMANY	2.85 M	2.3 M
AUSTRIA	380,000	145,000
GREECE	16,000	155,000
FRANCE	210,000	173,000
CZECHOSLOVAKIA	6,500	310,000
HUNGARY	750,000 (MILITARY AND CIVILIAN)	
ROMANIA	520,000	465,000
NETHERLANDS	13,500	236,300
BRITAIN	271,000	60,000
BELGIUM	9,500	75,000
ITALY	280,000	93,000
BULGARIA	18,500	1,500

◀ The changing border, which Winston Churchill described as an "iron curtain," between Soviet-dominated Eastern Europe and liberal democracies in the West.

ИМПЕРИАЛИЗМ— ЭТО ВОЙНА!

US

▲ "Imperialism is War!" A 1966 Soviet anti-Western propaganda poster that draws on the link, first made by Lenin, between capitalism and imperialism.

FALLING TEMPERATURE

As Soviet agents tried to put communists into positions of power throughout Eastern Europe, U.S. anxiety grew. In December 1945 this anxiety turned to alarm when pro-Soviet forces threatened to seize part of northern Iran. Although there was not yet a Cold War, the temperature was falling fast.

By the end of the year, some of Truman's advisers had begun to think of the Soviet Union as an enemy rather than as an ally. It was probably too late now to prevent the fissure between East and West from widening into an unbridgeable chasm.

WHOSE FAULT?

Some commentators blame both Stalin and Roosevelt for the coming of the Cold War. Stalin, they argue, deliberately rejected cooperation between East and West. Motivated by personal ambition, he set about imposing communism in Soviet-occupied countries and cynically ignored the wishes of those countries' inhabitants. These commentators accuse Roosevelt of appeasing Stalin. The Russian dictator only recognized brute force, they argue. By making concessions to Stalin early on, Roosevelt condemned millions of people to years of future tyranny.

Other commentators have been more inclined to blame Truman for the breakdown in relations between East and West. They accuse Truman of tactlessness and of failing to understand Soviet fears after the horrendous devastation of the war. These commentators argue that Soviet defensiveness was a response to aggressive U.S. capitalism. By 1945 the United States had captured a huge share of the world's trade, increasing Soviet fears of U.S. "economic imperialism." These fears would have been lessened, they suggest, if the United

States had not ended lend-lease to the Soviet Union immediately after the war.

The causes of the Cold War, however, cannot be explained simply in terms of the key personalities involved. The United States and the Soviet Union endorsed wholly different and conflicting ideologies. Since neither country was prepared to accept the merits of the other's ideology, harmony proved to be impossible. Both superpowers were also relatively inexperienced in global diplomacy and made many mistakes. During the war they failed to put together concrete postwar plans, and after the war they did not draft effective peace treaties. Since both countries had been forced into World War II by surprise attack, they also remained distrustful of potential enemies. Finally, a lopsided military balance — the Soviet Union had massive land forces, while the United States possessed sea and air superiority and nuclear weapons — created an atmosphere of mutual suspicion and hostility.

HARRY S. TRUMAN (1884–1972)

Truman worked his way up from farmworker, soldier, and failed shopkeeper to become a U.S. senator in 1935 and Roosevelt's vice president nine years later. When Truman became U.S. president in 1945, he had little experience in foreign affairs. He relied heavily upon his advisers and upon his strong sense of personal integrity. Although Truman was less flexible than Roosevelt and may have hastened the East-West rift, he provided the United States with firm leadership during the perilous early years of the Cold War.

▶ U.S. president Harry S. Truman, who in 1947 pledged U.S. support for "free peoples" in the face of what he perceived to be the advance of communist totalitarianism.

CHAPTER FOUR

Deep Freeze, 1946–1947

▲ Yugoslavia's communist leader Josip Tito (far right) with members of his Partisan Army of National Liberation, which fought a successful guerrilla campaign against the Nazis during World War II.

THE COMMUNIST ADVANCE

In 1946, former anti-Nazi guerrillas forcibly established communist governments in Albania and Yugoslavia without Moscow's direct support. Both governments, however, soon came under Stalin's influence, although in the case of Marshal Tito's Yugoslavia this influence only lasted until 1948.

Since there was no definitive agreement on the fate of Germany and Austria, each country remained divided into U.S., Soviet, British, and French zones of occupation. In the Soviet zones, communists were installed. The Soviets set about gaining complete control over those areas of Europe within their sphere of influence. Western journalists were prevented from reporting on events behind the Iron Curtain.

SOVIET DOMINATION

The Soviets understood that too obvious an intervention in a targeted country would alienate the local population and anger the West, so their tactics combined ruthlessness and stealth. First, they took local communists who had been exiled or imprisoned and placed them in key government positions — such as minister of justice or minister of the interior — to gain control over the country's police and security forces.

Next, the Soviets neutralized or eliminated influential opponents in politics, the media, and elsewhere. They did so through threats, false imprisonment, kidnapping, and even

THE SOVIET VIEW

In 1946, Nikolai Novikov, the Soviet Union's U.S. ambassador, had a very different interpretation of events in Eastern Europe than that of the West:

"Soviet armed forces are ... on the territory of Germany and other formerly hostile countries, thus guaranteeing that these countries will not ... again ... attack ... the USSR. In Bulgaria, Finland, Hungary, and Romania, democratic reconstruction has established regimes that ... maintain friendly relations with the USSR ... Poland, Czechoslovakia, and Yugoslavia [also have] democratic regimes ... that maintain relations with the USSR on the basis of ... friendship and mutual assistance."

murder. At the same time, they conducted massive pro-communist propaganda campaigns. In the last stage of their efforts, the Soviets declared the country a communist republic, often after elections in which they made sure the communists would win. Once Soviet-backed communists came into power, they were there to stay.

Members of Bulgaria's communist-backed "Fatherland Front" seized power on September 9, 1944. This coup put Bulgaria under Soviet influence for the next forty-six years.

THE TRIUMPH OF TERROR

After a communist-led coup in 1944, Bulgaria became a communist republic in 1946. In Romania, the Soviets backed a government that eliminated the opposition and forced out the country's monarch, and Romania became a communist republic in 1948. The United States protested in both cases and took a close interest in Poland, where Stalin had agreed to free elections. By the time elections were held, however, in January 1947, the opposition had been so weakened that the communists won eighty percent of the vote.

The Soviets had previously allowed elections in Hungary and Czechoslovakia before the communists had established themselves. In 1945, only seventeen percent of the Hungarian people voted communist. By 1949, however, terror tactics had transformed the country into a communist republic. In 1946, thirty-eight percent of the Czechoslovakian people voted communist and the party's popularity then declined. Yet in 1948, under the communist leader Gottwald, Czechoslovakia became a one-party communist state (see page 38).

▼ In 1946, George F. Kennan (below) sent his famous "long telegram" from Moscow. This telegram inspired the United States to take a much firmer line with the Soviets and helped foster the Cold War.

WAR OF WORDS

While the Soviet Union cemented its hold over Eastern Europe, its relationship with the United States quickly deteriorated. As often happened during the Cold War, this change resulted from words as much as from actions.

In February 1946, Stalin made a speech in which he repeated the Marxist belief that capitalism tended to produce wars. This viewpoint was hardly new — communist doctrine had always held that capitalists would use any means, including war, to increase their share of world markets. But a remark that might have been dismissed as merely tactless was regarded by the Truman administration as dangerously provocative. Could Stalin be suggesting that war between the United States and the Soviet Union was inevitable? To learn more, the U.S. government asked George Kennan, an expert in its Moscow embassy, for an analysis of Stalin's foreign policy.

Kennan replied with an 8,000-word telegram that influenced U.S. administrations for years to come. He claimed that Russia knew only one type of leadership — tyranny. Russian rulers, past and present, were terrified of outside influence on their country and would take any steps to combat it. The Soviets would not feel secure, Kennan insisted, until they had removed the threat of Western capitalism and liberal democracy.

CONTAINMENT

The "long telegram," as Kennan's message came to be known, became widely accepted in Washington, and those who disagreed with it no longer had Truman's ear. The time had come to get tough with the Soviets, Truman decided. The Soviet Union was like a cancer in the body, eating up the healthy tissue around it. To prevent disaster it had to be contained — and the only power capable of doing so was the United States.

Stalin knew nothing of the "long telegram," but he got a good idea of what one influential Westerner was thinking on March 5, 1946. On that day, Winston Churchill gave an address at Westminster College in Fulton, Missouri, in which he repeated his belief that an "iron curtain" had descended across Europe. Even some Westerners thought his remarks were too extreme, and the Soviets were furious. Only nine months earlier they had heralded Churchill as a staunch ally, but now they condemned him as a warmonger and a second Hitler. If you were to look for a specific point at which the Cold War began, this might be it.

THE LONG TELEGRAM

Kennan's "long telegram" painted the Soviet Union's policies in the darkest of colors. For example, he offered the following beliefs by Soviet leaders:

"A. Everything must be done to advance ... strength of USSR ... in international society. Conversely, no opportunity must be missed to reduce strength and influence ... of capitalist powers.

B. Soviet efforts ... must be directed toward deepening and exploiting of differences ... between capitalist powers. If these eventually deepen into an 'imperialist' war, this ... must be turned into revolutionary upheavals within ... capitalist countries."

▼ Winston Churchill in Fulton, Missouri, where he made his famous "iron curtain" speech in March 1946.

GETTING TOUGH

The United States first got tough over Iran. To prevent Nazi access to the country's oil fields, British and Soviet forces had occupied Iran during the war. By March of 1946 British forces had withdrawn, as agreed, but Soviet forces remained. The United States told the Soviet Union that deployment of its troops broke a clear agreement and might possibly lead to war.

The Iran situation was the first major confrontation of the Cold War to come before the newly formed United Nations (UN), and the outcome set a precedent. After face-saving talks, Stalin withdrew his troops. The Soviets repeated this tactic — i.e., pushing the East and West to the brink of war but always pulling back — many times during the Cold War.

▼ Shades of deception. Andrei Gromyko, Soviet representative to the United Nations, denies that the Soviet Union was behind the formation of a communist government in Czechoslovakia in 1948.

POWER OF VETO

Another precedent set by the Iran affair concerned the UN. The Security Council had been designed as the UN's main executive body, with the power to enforce decisions with military action, and comprised five permanent members (the

28

United States, the Soviet Union, Britain, France, and China) as well as ten elected members. When the UN was organized, Stalin insisted that each permanent member be given veto power over all decisions, to prevent the Western democracies from voting together against the Soviet Union.

This veto rendered the Council impotent without U.S.-Soviet cooperation. When U.S. secretary of state James Byrnes used the UN to publicly attack the Soviets on Iran, Soviet representative Andrei Gromyko simply walked out. The issue, like many to come, was settled not by the international community but by politicians in Washington and Moscow.

"STAYING HERE"

The United States soon showed its new stance again. In May of 1946, it banned the Soviet Union from collecting war reparations from the U.S. zone of occupation in Germany, and at a peace conference in Paris it resisted Soviet demands — which were supported by the French — to permanently partition Germany. When the issue could not be resolved, Secretary of State Byrnes announced that U.S. troops would remain in Germany. "We will not shirk our duty," he told an audience in Stuttgart, a German city in the U.S. zone. "We are staying here."

Later, the Soviets sought access to the Mediterranean for their Black Sea fleet. When the Turks refused to allow them passage, Soviet troops gathered on the Turkish border. The United States then sent warships off the coast of Turkey, and the Soviet fleet stayed in the Black Sea.

▲ U.S. secretary of state James F. Byrnes, shown here signing President Truman's official declaration that the Second World War is over, played a key role in the Truman administration's decision to maintain a U.S. military presence in Europe.

STANDING FIRM

The Iranian crisis centered around the Tudeh, a Soviet-backed party in the Iranian province of Azerbaijan. When the Soviets allowed Iranian troops into Azerbaijan, U.S. ambassador to Iran George Allen told Under Secretary of State Dean Acheson why the United States had triumphed:

"In the Iranian view the quick collapse of the Tudeh Party was due to the conviction of everyone — the Russians, the Iranians, and the Azerbaijanis — that the United States was not bluffing but solidly supporting Iranian sovereignty." He concluded that *"Iran is no stronger than the UN and the UN, in the last analysis, is no stronger than the U.S."*

One man, one vote. Stalin (left) and Molotov cast votes in the election for the Supreme Soviet in February 1947. The election for this constituency was won by V. I. Dikushin, the only candidate allowed to run.

STALIN'S MOTIVES

By January 1947, the Soviet Union had twice backed down in the face of U.S. resolve. It did so in part because Stalin wanted to avoid a war he could not win. By 1948 the United States had tested numerous nuclear weapons, and these tests had served as warnings that a war between the United States and the Soviet Union would lead to the destruction of many Russian cities — a scenario that even Stalin's iron-fisted dictatorship could probably not survive.

Stalin may also have backed down because he never intended to go to war in the first place. No evidence exists that he planned to attack the West, and his saber rattling was probably meant to scare off the United States rather than goad it into conflict. If this is true, then Kennan's concern (see page 26) that Stalin hoped to destroy capitalism by force was mistaken, and the U.S. policy of "containing" Soviet expansion was probably also somewhat misguided.

STALIN'S RESPONSE

Churchill's "iron curtain" speech drew an immediate response from Stalin, who, in an interview he gave to the Soviet newspaper *Pravda*, once again emphasized the defensive nature of Soviet foreign policy:

"[Is it surprising that] the Soviet Union, in a desire to ensure its security … , tries to [ensure that Eastern Europe] should have governments whose relations to the Soviet Union are loyal? How can one … qualify these peaceful aspirations of the USSR as 'expansionist tendencies'? … Communism … grew because during the hard years of … fascism in Europe, Communists showed themselves to be reliable, daring and self-sacrificing fighters … for the liberty of peoples."

THE CIRCLE OF FEAR

The Cold War was essentially a product of fear. Stalin feared the economic and nuclear might of the United States; he feared, as always, for the security of his own position; he also feared that a reunited and revived Germany, supported by its new allies, would attack Russia again. In response to these fears, he acted ruthlessly to surround the Soviet Union with a shield of subservient communist states.

The United States and their allies noted Stalin's aggression and took his talk of communist world domination at face value. Frightened, they responded with a policy of Soviet containment. This policy only increased Stalin's fears, prompting him to adopt a still more aggressive stance. Thus began a vicious circle of fear and misunderstanding that neither side was able to break.

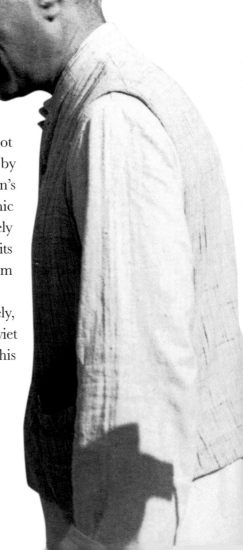

BRITISH WITHDRAWAL

The next stage in the Cold War's escalation was not triggered by U.S. or Soviet aggression but rather by Britain's continuing problems. In early 1947, Britain's Labour government was faced with a catastrophic economic crisis, and it decided to cut back immediately on overseas commitments. Britain would grant India its independence as swiftly as possible, withdraw from Palestine, and cut all aid to Greece and Turkey.

The Truman administration reacted immediately, determined that the United States, and not the Soviet Union, would fill the power vacuum created by this British retreat from the world stage.

▶ Leader of the world's largest democracy. Jawaharlal Nehru, India's first freely elected prime minister, in August 1947. During the Second World War, Nehru had been sympathetic to the Allied cause but had refused to cooperate with Britain.

31

CHAPTER FIVE

Containment and Security

DEMOCRATS AND REPUBLICANS

Unlike Stalin, President Truman was not free to draw up foreign policy and implement it as he wished. The Constitution guarantees a balance of power between the president and Congress. For example, while the president commands the armed forces, Congress declares war, and it is also responsible for raising taxes and allocating spending. In February 1947, Truman's problem was that he needed Congressional approval to fund his foreign policy.

Truman belonged to the Democratic Party, but in the November 1946 elections, the Republican Party had won control of both the Senate and the House of Representatives for the first time since 1928. The new conservative mood in Congress reflected the American people's desire to get back to normal, now that the war was over. After World War I ended in 1918, the United States put its own house in order and let the rest of the world sort itself out, and many Americans

▼ From world war to civil war. Members of Greece's communist-controlled National Liberation Front (EAM), an anti-Nazi resistance movement, refused to disarm after German withdrawal. Below, EAM prisoners being led away to Gaol in 1944.

wanted to do the same now. Republican politicians promised to "bring the boys (U.S. troops still overseas) home."

THE ROTTEN APPLE

The news that Britain planned to end its aid to Greece and Turkey ran through the White House like an electric shock. Turkey lay along the southwest border of the Soviet Union and was the strategic key to the vital oil reserves of the Middle East. In Greece, a civil war was raging between communists backed by Yugoslovian leader Tito (the United States wrongly believed that they were being supported by the Soviets) and pro-Westerners led by the king. Both countries, the Truman administration decided, had to be kept within the Western sphere of influence. First, however, the Republican Congress had to be persuaded to fund further overseas commitments.

Truman, accompanied by his new secretary of state, the upright and plain-speaking George C. Marshall, as well as Under Secretary of State Dean Acheson, invited congressional leaders to a meeting in the White House on February 28, 1947. At a vital moment in the discussions, Acheson used the metaphor of one rotten apple spoiling a barrel of apples: If the communists won control of Greece, he explained, the corruption would spread from this one rotten apple eastwards to Iran and beyond, south into the Middle East and Africa, and west into Italy and France. If the United States allowed this corruption to spread, before long the country would stand alone against a communist world bent on its destruction. His audience was completely convinced of his argument.

▲ President Truman presents the Distinguished Service Medal to General George C. Marshall. Marshall served as U.S. secretary of state from 1947 to 1949 and is remembered for his "Marshall Plan," which provided aid to postwar Western Europe.

MIKHAILOVICH MOLOTOV (1890–1986)

An ally of Stalin since before the Russian Revolution, Molotov played a key role in Soviet foreign affairs from 1939 to 1949. He negotiated the Non-aggression Pact with the Nazis (1939) and the alliance with Britain (1942), and he stood at Stalin's side at Tehran, Yalta, and Potsdam. After the war he organized the pacts that bound the states of Eastern Europe to the Soviet Union. He was uncompromising over Germany and became famous for saying "no" to countless United Nations proposals.

CONGRESS LISTENS

On March 12, 1947, Truman appeared before Congress and asked for $400 million in aid for Greece and Turkey. It was a moment of great drama. The president, a powerful speaker, put his argument in the plainest possible terms, as a simple question of good versus evil. He presented the United States as the champion of freedom against oppression and of democracy against tyranny.

Truman reminded Congress of what happened when the United States shirked its international responsibilities after the First World War, allowing fascism and communism to flourish. The country, he said, had a moral duty to take over active leadership of the free world, and he hoped U.S. money would be made available to combat poverty overseas, for "the seeds of totalitarian regimes ... spread and grow in the evil soil of poverty and strife." He proclaimed that by supporting "free peoples" everywhere, the United States would both prevent future conflict and, in time, boost the international capitalist system on which America's prosperity depended. Communism, he said, must go "no farther."

▲ President Truman addressing Congress on March 12, 1947. He is setting out the terms of what became known as the "Truman Doctrine," which held that the United States should not withdraw into isolation.

THE TRUMAN DOCTRINE

When President Truman appeared before Congress on March 12, 1947, he outlined his view of the new Cold War world:

"At the present moment ... nearly every nation must choose between alternative ways of life ...

"One ... is based upon the will of the majority, and is distinguished by free institutions, representative government, [and] ... freedom of speech.

"The second ... is based upon the will of a minority forcibly imposed upon the majority. It relies upon terror and oppression."

THE TRUMAN DOCTRINE

Truman won the day and Congress voted for the aid he requested. The acceptance of what came to be known as the "Truman Doctrine" marked a major turning point in American foreign policy. In a sense, the doctrine confirmed the role that the United States had been edging towards since the end of the war. There was no guarantee, however, that active U.S. intervention in Europe and elsewhere would continue. Public opinion had kept America out of World War II for two years, and despite growing hostility towards the Soviet Union, there were plenty of signs in early 1947 that the American people had grown tired of foreign adventures.

Now Truman, Congress, and many commentators in the media were asking Americans to think again. The rest of the free world needed them, the American people were told. They responded to the challenge — real or imaginary — and the Truman Doctrine guided the U.S. view of the world for at least the next twenty-five years.

The United States, Truman said, would now assist all "free peoples … resisting attempted subjugation by armed minorities or by outside pressures" and would contain communism behind its iron curtain. Greece and Turkey were the first states to benefit. In other, more powerful countries, however, the need for American help was almost as pressing.

▼ Dollar power. U.S. supplies, draped in the Stars and Stripes to make it clear where they came from, arrive in Greece in August 1947.

THE CONDITION OF EUROPE

World War II exacted a horrendous toll on Europe. Some thirty million people had been killed and perhaps sixty million driven from their homes. The widespread destruction of property on the continent had also been devastating.

In 1945, only about seventy-seven percent of Europe's available farmland was being utilized. German industrial production had fallen to about fifteen percent of its pre-war level, and the French and Italian transport systems lay in ruins. Europe was a vast wasteland full of shattered homes, shops, factories, roads, railways, bridges, and even entire cities. Recovery was painfully slow and in some places nonexistent.

Europe provided ample evidence for Truman's belief that misery was the breeding ground for anti-Western regimes. By 1947 half of Europe was already communist. Czechoslovakia was the only country behind the Iron Curtain without a communist government. The popularity of the French Communist Party appeared to be undermining the newly established Fourth Republic, while the Italian Communist Party, the largest outside of

▼ The ruins of Monte Cassino, Italy, which had witnessed some of the most bitter and destructive fighting of World War II. Similar scenes were common throughout Europe after the war.

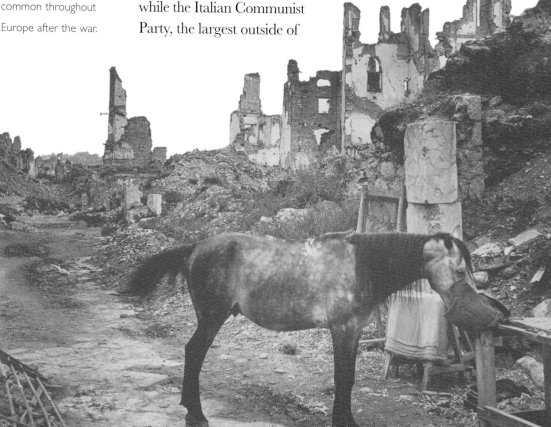

Eastern Europe, had a chance of winning the Italian elections scheduled for April 1948. If the United States wanted to safeguard liberal democracy in Europe, it would have to do more than keep forces there — it would have to help the continent become prosperous again. The man who saw this most clearly was U.S. secretary of state George C. Marshall.

THE MARSHALL PLAN

Marshall unveiled his European Recovery Program, or "Marshall Plan," in a speech at Harvard University on June 5, 1947. He initially proposed that the United States provide $17 billion in aid, which would take the form of loans and also grants that included money, food, and machinery.

Every country in Europe was invited to apply for the aid. The Soviet Union showed some interest, but when Stalin learned of U.S. plans to rebuild Germany he condemned the program as a capitalist plot, and he responded by creating the Communist Bureau of Information (Cominform), an anti-Western alliance of communist parties. When Poland and Czechoslovakia showed interest in U.S. aid, Stalin threatened to use force against them and they backed off. No other Eastern European country applied.

The size of the aid package alarmed Congress. Although it voted small grants, protracted negotiations over approval of the main package lasted into 1948. The program's opponents questioned whether the communist threat was real or imagined. In February 1948 they got their answer, when Czechoslovakia became a communist country.

▲ Funding the German miracle. This poster reads "It's making progress — with the Marshall Plan," around the slogan "Building work."

POLITICAL AID

U.S. under secretary of state Dean Acheson announced what became known as the Marshall Plan in a speech in May 1947. The speech was widely reported in Europe but not in the United States. Its restatement by Secretary of State Marshall a month later, emphasizing the plan's political aim, received widespread coverage on both sides of the Atlantic:

"Our policy is directed against hunger, poverty, despair, and chaos. Its purpose should be the revival of a working economy in the world so as to permit the growth of conditions in which free governments can exist."

▲ Czechoslovakia's new communist prime minister, Klement Gottwald, reviews a parade of armed militia in February 1948. The communist takeover in Czechoslovakia was partly the result of the United States' inflexibility.

CZECHOSLOVAKIA

The coalition government that formed in Czechoslovakia after elections in May 1946 included communists, but they were not in the majority. President Benes and Foreign Minister Masaryk tried to steer a middle course between East and West, and they were bitterly disappointed when Stalin's threats forced them to cancel their application for Marshall aid. Later, Masaryk asked the United States for food to help his country through the hard winter of 1947–48, but his request was unwisely rejected because of his apparent anti-American stance. Stalin immediately offered Czechoslovakia 600,000 tons of grain.

In February 1948, non-communist members of the Czech government resigned, in the hopes that Benes would call fresh elections in which the communists would be defeated. Faced with communist-organized rallies, however, Benes lost his nerve and asked communist leader Klement Gottwald to form a provisional government. When elections were held in May only communists were allowed to run. Czechoslovakia was now behind the Iron Curtain, where it remained for forty years.

THE LIFELINE

The Truman Administration used the communist takeover in Czechoslovakia to whip up anti-Soviet fervor, and a frightened Congress approved $5.3 billion in aid for Europe almost immediately. More aid followed over the next four years, until the total had reached over $13 billion.

British foreign secretary Ernest Bevin described Marshall aid as a "lifeline to a drowning man." Although economists today disagree on exactly how important a role the aid played in Europe's recovery, all countries certainly benefited, and in some countries, such as Greece, U.S. assistance was vital. Marshall's program also boosted the American economy. The

U.S. government bought food for Europe from American farms, and it bought machinery, such as tractors and lathes, for Europe from American manufacturers. Even money given to European countries as grants and loans benefitted the U.S. economy, since much of the money was spent on goods only available from the United States.

The Marshall Plan also had important political consequences. It accelerated and hardened the division of Eastern and Western Europe by forcing countries to choose between Soviet and U.S. support. France and Italy came firmly into the Western sphere, while Czechoslovakia, Poland, Yugoslavia, and Finland remained outside. In Western Europe, the business of organizing Marshall aid sowed seeds of cooperation that grew into the European Economic Community and, later, into the European Union.

PEACE-MONGERING

▲ An American cartoon from 1947 suggests how Marshall aid would keep Western Europe outside the Soviet sphere of influence.

MARSHALL AID

This graph shows the massive scale of Marshall aid, which totalled the modern equivalent of almost $140 billion. To avoid the problem of debt, which crippled Europe after World War I, 80% of the aid was given as grants.

MARSHALL PLAN AID TO WESTERN EUROPE
IN MILLIONS (M) AND BILLIONS (B) OF U.S. DOLLARS

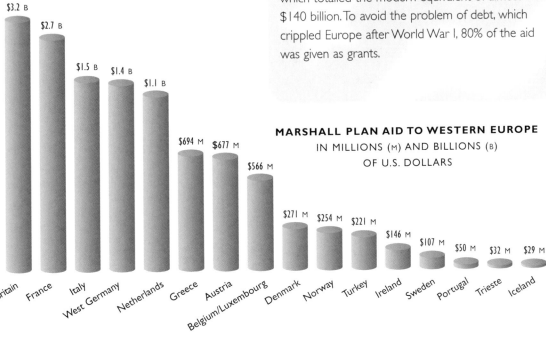

$3.2 B — Britain
$2.7 B — France
$1.5 B — Italy
$1.4 B — West Germany
$1.1 B — Netherlands
$694 M — Greece
$677 M — Austria
$566 M — Belgium/Luxembourg
$271 M — Denmark
$254 M — Norway
$221 M — Turkey
$146 M — Ireland
$107 M — Sweden
$50 M — Portugal
$32 M — Trieste
$29 M — Iceland

CRISIS IN BERLIN

At Yalta, Potsdam, and Paris, the Allies had failed to agree on a final settlement for Germany. They did, however, agree on three intermediate developments. First, land to the east of the Oder and Neisse Rivers was to be given to Poland. Second, Germany to the west of these rivers was to be divided into Soviet, U.S., and British zones of occupation. (The French later insisted upon, and received, a fourth zone.) Lastly, Germany was to undergo the "three Ds": demilitarization, denazification, and democratization.

WHOSE DEMOCRACY?

While the Soviets and the Western democracies agreed on denazification, the issue of Germany's demilitarization and, in particular, democratization led to a rift between the two sides. For the West, "democratization" meant establishing Germany as a liberal democracy supported by a capitalist economy. For the Soviet Union, however, "democratization" meant installing a Soviet-style communist government with tight control of the economy. The two approaches were incompatible.

The first clash came in May 1946, when the United States stopped the Soviets from collecting reparation payments from the U.S. zone. Tensions escalated further in September, when Truman announced that U.S. forces would remain in Germany indefinitely. Then, in January 1947, the U.S. and British zones united to form "Bizonia." The French zone made it "Trizonia" in March 1948. With talented refugees from the East and Marshall Plan aid, the Western zones recovered fast.

A DIVIDED CITY

Attention now focused on Berlin, deep within the Soviet zone. The capital city was divided into an eastern Soviet sector

▼ This map shows the zones of occupation in Germany after the war, as well as the three vital air corridors between Berlin and the West.

Key

Areas occupied by:
- ☐ Soviet Union
- ☐ Britain
- ☐ United States
- ☐ France

and western U.S., British, and French sectors. Stalin feared this armed, capitalist enclave behind the Iron Curtain and wished to have it removed.

In June of 1947, Berliners elected an anti-communist mayor, Ernst Reuter, but his authority was immediately denied in the Soviet sector. The following February, the Western democracies met privately to discuss Germany's future. Angry at being shut out of this discussion, the Soviets left the Allied Control Council, which supervised German affairs.

Matters came to a head in June 1948, when the Western powers agreed to change the currency in Trizonia and West Berlin from the reichsmark to the new deutsche mark. The Soviets objected and stepped up their harassment of road, rail, and canal links to West Berlin. Soviet harassment soon became a total blockade. The survival of two and a half million West Berliners was now in question.

▲ Tempelhof, one of West Berlin's three airports. From August 1948 to May 1949, West Berlin's airports were its only link to the Western world.

RUSSIA'S FEARS

Marshal Zhukov, writing to Stalin from Berlin on May 24, 1946, advises the Soviet government to reject an American draft treaty for the demilitarization of Germany. The letter shows how, less than a year after the end of the war, a chasm of suspicion and mistrust had opened between the former allies.

"Workers of the world, Unite!

"In my view the real purpose of the draft treaty is:

- *a wish to end the occupation of Germany and to get Soviet forces out of there as quickly as possible … ;*

- *a wish to hinder sending … reparations from Germany to the USSR;*

- *a wish to keep Germany as a base for future aggression against us."*

Property of
Waterloo High School

German "rubble-women," earning 1.20 deutsche mark an hour and a hot meal for every shift, help build a new airport for West Berlin at Tegel in August 1948.

AIRLIFT

On June 24, 1948, the Soviets announced that Berlin's four-power administration was over and the Western powers had no right to be in the city. The Soviets' intention was clear: the Western enclave of Berlin would be destroyed through starvation.

West Berlin was of little strategic value to the Western democracies. The Soviet threat, however, posed a real challenge to the Truman Doctrine and U.S. resolve. The United States and its allies responded immediately to the blockade.

On June 26, 1948, the United States and Britain began the "Berlin airlift," flying food and other vital supplies into the city's Western sector and carrying refugees and industrial exports back out to the West. For eleven months, hundreds of aircraft shuttled back and forth along the 265-mile (426-kilometer) air corridors linking Berlin to West Germany. At the height of the airlift, at least thirty aircraft were in the air at any one time. Thanks to the 2.3 million tons of supplies brought in by these planes, West Berlin managed to survive the Soviet blockade.

During the airlift, both sides built up their forces as if preparing for war. By mid-July the Soviets had forty divisions in Germany. The United States had only eight, but the divisions were backed by U.S. strategic bombers, purportedly armed with atomic bombs. Here was the first classic Cold War standoff: military buildups and threats without actual conflict.

STALIN RELENTS

The Soviets dared not attack the Western supply planes for fear of sparking war. They were also frustrated by the West's disruption of communications in East Germany and hurt by a Western embargo on exports from the Eastern bloc. On May 12, 1949, they accepted the inevitable and lifted the blockade. Fearing the blockade might be reimposed, the West continued to stockpile supplies in West Berlin for another four months.

The Berlin blockade was the first great crisis of the Cold War. It confirmed both the East-West rift and the U.S. military commitment in Europe. It also altered the way the West saw Germany. The West Germans were now friends and allies, while the East Germans and the Soviets were the new villains. This view became a political reality with the establishment of the pro-Western German Federal Republic in September 1949 and the creation of the Soviet-dominated German Democratic Republic a month later.

▼ A crowd of West Berliners watches anxiously as a U.S. plane comes in to land with a cargo of vital supplies. At the height of the airlift, a plane was taking off and landing in West Berlin every ninety seconds.

THE BERLIN AIRLIFT IN DETAIL

★ DURATION: JUNE 24, 1948, TO MAY 12, 1949

★ NUMBER OF FLIGHTS (UNITED STATES): 189,963

★ NUMBER OF FLIGHTS (BRITAIN): 87,841

★ NUMBER OF FLIGHTS (FRANCE): 424

★ NUMBER OF PASSENGERS BROUGHT IN: 61,100

★ NUMBER OF PASSENGERS TAKEN OUT: 67,900

★ TOTAL COST: $224,000,000

★ WEIGHT OF SUPPLIES BROUGHT IN: 2,323,738 TONS

★ WEIGHT OF EXPORTS TRANSPORTED TO THE WEST: 2,500 TONS

★ CASUALTIES (UNITED STATES): 31

★ CASUALTIES (BRITAIN): 39

CHAPTER SIX

Hot War

PREPARATIONS FOR WAR

By the time the Berlin crisis began, there was a real possibility that U.S.-Soviet hostility might boil over into outright war. The United States took various steps to deter such a war, but it also made preparations to win the war if those steps failed.

By 1947, the United States had reorganized its armed forces under the Joint Chiefs of Staff and a secretary of defense. The National Military Establishment Act combined the War and Navy Departments, made the Air Force a separate entity, and gave the Strategic Air Command control over the planes that would carry atomic bombs. In 1948, sixty of these bombers, B-29 "Superfortresses," were flown to bases in Britain. The planes were not armed with atomic weapons, though few knew this at the time.

At the height of the Berlin crisis, in 1949, President Truman announced that the United States was sending military aid to Western Europe. Three months later, the United States,

▼ The might of America. Boeing B-17s, or "Flying Fortresses," on a raid over Japan during World War II. Before the long-range missile was introduced, the bomber was the primary offensive weapon of the United States and the only means for delivering nuclear weapons.

Canada, Britain, and nine European nations signed a treaty establishing the North Atlantic Treaty Organization (NATO). This treaty bound NATO members to come to each other's aid if attacked. The message from a united West to the Soviet Union was clear: hands off.

The Soviets, meanwhile, had been developing their own nuclear weapons, and in August 1949 they secretly detonated their first atomic bomb. When the West learned of the test, the impact was dramatic. In military terms, the United States had lost its ace of spades, and the age of nuclear terror had begun.

THE CIA

The Central Intelligence Agency, or CIA, was established by the National Security Act of 1947 to collect, coordinate, and analyze U.S. foreign intelligence, and it became the heart of U.S. espionage during the Cold War. Under presidential control, it was primarily concerned with infiltrating the Soviet system to get advance warning of Soviet technological advances, military deployment, and political initiatives. The CIA's activities were first promoted as necessary for the defense of the "free world," but when they came under widespread public scrutiny in the mid-1960s, its reputation was severely tarnished.

CHINA

The news coming out of China did little to lighten the United States' gloom. Not long after Japan's surrender, the CCP and KMT had resumed their bitter civil war (see pages 14 and 15). Despite $2 billion of U.S. aid, Chiang Kai-shek's KMT squandered its early advances. By the summer of 1949, the communist forces of Mao Tse-Tung controlled the most populous country on earth.

The communist victory in China was a serious blow to the Truman administration. Far from containing communism, it had actually presided over communism's massive expansion. (Interestingly, however, Mao received very little backing from Stalin, who for a long time regarded Mao as nothing more than a rebellious peasant.) Wherever communism threatened next, therefore, Truman was determined to resist it with all the force he could muster.

▶ Mao Tse-Tung, China's charismatic communist leader. His seizure of power in 1949 had not been widely predicted, even in the Soviet Union.

CHINA

Yalu River

NORTH KOREA

Chongju

Pyongyang

Panmumjom

Inchon

Seoul

SOUTH KOREA

Taejon

Yellow Sea

furthest extent of communist advance

Pusan

Soviet Union

Sea of Japan

armistice line, 1953

38th parallel

JAPAN

0   150 mi

0   300 km

▲ After World War II, Korea split in half. The two sides fought each other during the Korean War of 1950–1953.

KOREA DIVIDED

During World War II, Korea, a Japanese colony since 1910, suffered extremely harsh treatment by the Japanese. In 1943, the United States, Britain, and Chiang Kai-shek's China agreed that Korean independence would be an official Allied war aim.

When the Soviet Union declared war on Japan in August 1945, however, Red Army divisions moved swiftly through Japanese-occupied Manchuria and into northern Korea. The United States, afraid that all of Korea would fall into Soviet hands, suggested the country be divided between U.S. and Soviet occupation forces. At the time there were no U.S. troops in Korea, but surprisingly the Soviets accepted the U.S. proposal and the Red Army duly halted along the 38th parallel. Since Korea has no natural obstacles, such as a mountain range, dividing north from south, this line of latitude was a completely artificial divide. A few weeks later, U.S. forces took up positions south of the new border.

STANDOFF

In December 1945, the United States and the Soviet Union signed an agreement for administering Korea and returning the country to independence, but little progress was made. The Korean situation resembled partitioned Germany, where each side feared that withdrawal would lead to takeover by the other side. So the Koreans, who had no wish to live in a divided land, became the latest victims of the escalating Cold War.

For the next four years North Korea was ruled by the Soviet-backed leader Kim Il Sung, while South Korea was governed by Syngman Rhee, who had U.S. support. As Kim eliminated non-communist opposition and established a

DEFENSE SPENDING

The Cold War crises of 1949–1950 had a dramatic effect on U.S. military spending. By 1951, America's defense budget was greater than the budgets of all other Eastern and Western powers put together. As weapons became more technologically sophisticated, and therefore more expensive, year after year, the United States' wealth gave it a massive advantage over the Soviet Union.

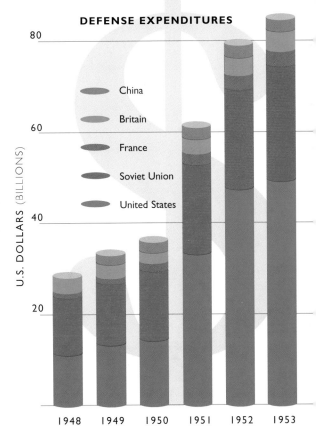

DEFENSE EXPENDITURES

- China
- Britain
- France
- Soviet Union
- United States

U.S. DOLLARS (BILLIONS)

80
60
40
20

1948 1949 1950 1951 1952 1953

socialist economy, large numbers of Koreans fled to South Korea, where capitalism (and corruption) flourished. Tensions remained high at the north-south border, but by June 1949 both Soviet and U.S. forces had withdrawn, leaving the Koreans to sort out their differences for themselves.

KIM'S REQUEST

Soviet nuclear testing and the communist triumph in China sharply refocused U.S. foreign policy. The White House ordered the development of a new type of nuclear weapon, the hydrogen bomb. To build up conventional, nonnuclear U.S. forces, it also requested a five-fold increase in military expenditures to $50 billion.

The Soviets and Chinese, meanwhile, signed the Treaty of Friendship, Alliance, and Mutual Assistance in February 1950. This treaty strengthened the Soviet position in Asia, and Stalin began to take seriously Kim's repeated suggestion that North Korea complete the communist takeover of the Korean peninsula.

▼ The Sino-Soviet Treaty of Friendship, Alliance, and Mutual Assistance is signed in February 1950. This photograph is one of few to show Stalin and Mao (left to right in back left corner, in idealized poses) together, but their images may have been added to the picture for propaganda purposes.

"Remember June 25th, the day the communists invaded" reads the text of this propaganda poster issued by the government of South Korea.

KIM'S ATTACK

The Korean War began on June 25, 1950, with a massive North Korean attack over the 38th parallel. Armed with Soviet weapons and tanks, the 100,000-strong communist forces reached the South Korean capital of Seoul in three days. The United States immediately sent troops commanded by General Douglas MacArthur, an outspoken World War II veteran, to aid South Korea. It also urged the United Nations to intervene against North Korean aggression.

The UN's Security Council decided to form a UN force to aid the South Koreans. Since the Soviets were boycotting the UN to protest its exclusion of communist China, they were not present to veto this decision. North Korea would ultimately face South Korean and U.S. troops, as well as UN troops from a sixteen-nation coalition that included Britain, Australia, and New Zealand.

DOUGLAS MACARTHUR (1880–1964)

A brilliant yet controversial soldier and administrator, MacArthur was decorated 13 times during World War I, and during World War II he masterminded the Allied advance across the Pacific. After the war, he commanded the Allied forces occupying Japan and was virtually the country's leader. He initially commanded U.S. troops during the Korean War, but his disagreement with the Truman administration over the war's direction led to his dismissal by Truman in 1951. The following year MacArthur failed to be nominated as a candidate for the U.S. presidency.

PUSAN AND INCHON

At first, UN-U.S. forces fared no better than the South Koreans. They were defeated at Taejon and driven southwest to a territory around the city of Pusan. While U.S. aircraft bombed North Korean supply lines, MacArthur gathered his forces behind the Naktong River for a counterattack.

MacArthur struck on September 15, 1950. He combined a frontal assault with a seaborne landing at Inchon, 150 miles (241 km) behind enemy lines, that was the largest of its kind since the Allied invasion of Normandy in World War II. The offensive was a success. After UN and U.S. forces reached Seoul on September 26, they advanced to the 38th parallel.

STRIKING NORTH

The United States believed that North Korean aggression was part of a Soviet plan for world domination. While this view may have been misguided — Stalin was actually just backing an aggressive ally — the original U.S. objective in South Korea had been to contain communism.

With MacArthur and South Korean leader Rhee urging pursuit of the retreating North Koreans over the 38th parallel, that objective changed. The United States was now tempted to reunite all of Korea under a U.S.-backed government. MacAthur was allowed to advance into North Korea.

Furious at North Korea's failure, Stalin withdrew most Soviet advisers. On October 19, MacArthur captured the North Korean capital of Pyongyang. He then drove towards the Yalu River and the Chinese border, where U.S. troops captured enemy soldiers who did not understand their Korean interrogators. The reason why? They were actually Chinese.

▼ U.S. marines advancing towards Inchon after their successful seaborne landing behind enemy lines five days earlier. Technically, U.S. forces fought for the United Nations.

ENTER CHINA

Neither Stalin nor Mao wanted to commit forces in Korea. Mao, however, would not accept UN-U.S. troops on his border, and he dropped diplomatic hints that they should withdraw. When the United States ignored these hints, Mao sent "volunteers" to assist the North Koreans. It was some of these Chinese soldiers who had been captured. The Chinese troops inflicted a sharp defeat on UN-U.S. forces, then withdrew.

Mao's message was clear: pull back or face more of the same. MacArthur, however, still did not believe he had been fighting the Chinese and refused to pull back. On November 26, 1950, Mao responded with a huge attack, led by the experienced General Peng De-Huai, that sent the UN-U.S. forces reeling backwards.

ADVANCE AND RETREAT

What the Chinese army lacked in airpower and heavy weapons, it more than made up for in sheer numbers and personal bravery. The UN-U.S. troops were simply overwhelmed by wave after wave of advancing Chinese.

▼ A communist artillery team attacking UN-U.S. positions during the Korean War. Chinese-North Korean offensives rocked the UN-U.S. forces, who initially underestimated the enemy's military power.

The communists retook Pyongyang on December 6 and captured Seoul a month later. In February 1951, UN-U.S. forces launched a counterattack. By late March, they had returned to the 38th parallel, where they managed to withstand a huge Chinese counteroffensive.

TO BOMB OR NOT TO BOMB?

China's intervention deeply concerned President Truman, who feared all-out war with China might lead to war with the Soviet Union. He insisted, therefore, that the conflict should remain a limited operation. MacArthur, passionately anti-communist, demanded complete U.S. involvement that included the bombing of Chinese cities. In April 1951 Truman replaced him with another distinguished World War II veteran, General Matthew B. Ridgeway.

STALEMATE

With the front line stabilized near the point where it had begun, the conflict reached a stalemate. A political solution, unfortunately, proved as elusive as a military one. Talks broke down on several occasions, leading to fresh hostilities.

Few gains were made on the ground, where both sides had adopted strong defensive positions. U.S. bombers, however, pounded North Korean supply routes, factories, and cities. The weight of bombs dropped on North Korea was only slightly less than what was dropped on Germany during the entire course of World War II.

A LESSON OF SUPREME IMPORTANCE

The success of Chinese forces in the Korean War took many Western observers by surprise. The delighted Chinese, as this propaganda report in September of 1953 shows, insisted the war should encourage all colonies to fight for independence:

"It is a lesson whose international meaning is of supreme importance. It proves beyond all doubt that the time when a Western aggressor could occupy a country… has gone forever. It proves that a nation, once aroused, which dares to rise and fight for its glory, its independence, and the safety of the fatherland, is invincible."

▼ Bomber power. Napalm attacks by U.S. B-26 bombers devastate North Korean supply lines in 1950.

▲ One soldier to another. President-elect Eisenhower (left, seated), who commanded the Allied forces in Europe from 1944 to 1945, shares rations with U.S. troops in Korea in 1951. Eisenhower talked tough but stopped short of attacking positions within China.

DWIGHT EISENHOWER (1890–1969)

Eisenhower had a remarkable ability to get along well with almost everyone he met. He put this talent to good use during World War II, when he was supreme commander of Allied forces and oversaw the D-Day invasion of Normandy and the advance into Germany. After the war, Eisenhower commanded NATO land forces, and in 1952 he was elected president of the United States. During his two terms of office he showed moderation in foreign affairs, resisting demands that the United States be more aggressive towards communism.

ARMISTICE

In November 1952, Republican Dwight Eisenhower was elected U.S. president. A careful yet committed anti-communist, he sought to end the war on terms favorable to the United States. In May 1953 he stated that the Chinese capital of Beijing might be subject to a U.S. nuclear attack.

Eisenhower's threat, however, was not necessary. Stalin had died in March 1953, and the new Soviet administration had already decided to end the war. As Mao Tse-Tung had reached the same decision, an armistice was signed on July 27, 1953, which created a new border between North and South Korea that was buffered by a demilitarized zone.

THE COST

Neither side had made significant territorial gains. Korea remained a place divided by fear and hatred. Many of its larger cities and towns were in ruins. Perhaps five million of its people had become refugees, most of whom fled from North Korea to South Korea.

The casualties on both sides, civilian and military, were horrific. Nearly a million North Koreans and perhaps 600,000 South Koreans lost their lives. The Chinese dead may have totalled half a million. A total of 57,000 UN soldiers and airmen were killed, 54,000 of whom were American. A further 100,000 Americans were wounded.

COLD WAR

The Korean conflict had a major impact on the Cold War. In the United States, it fueled hatred for communism and reinforced the view that the Soviets and Chinese sought world domination. In addition, the United States mistakenly believed that its nuclear threat had helped end the conflict, so the country built up its nuclear arsenal after the war. The United States also believed that after holding back the communists in Korea, it could do the same elsewhere — a belief that would eventually lead to U.S. involvement in Vietnam.

After the war, the Soviets made sure that the United States never again acted under a UN umbrella. Not until the Gulf War in 1991, after the collapse of Soviet communism, would the UN again take military action against an aggressor (Iraq).

The war also brought Japan firmly into alliance with the West. The billions of dollars spent by the U.S. military in Japan boosted the Japanese economy. Eventually, most of Southeast Asia benefited from Japan's postwar economic miracle.

Lastly, the war damaged relations between China and the Soviet Union. Stalin had offered to provide China with all the weapons it needed — as long as it paid for them. Mao was angered by this lack of communist fraternity, and the friendship with his northern neighbor cooled.

▼ U.S. troops advance to the front as South Korean women flee to safety on the other side of the road. Success against communism in Korea helped motivate U.S. involvement in Vietnam twelve years later.

CHAPTER SEVEN

The Balance of Terror

THE PASSING OF STALIN

The year 1953 marked no sharp break in the history of the Cold War, but with the death of Stalin and the end of the Korean War a turning point had been reached. Stalin had kept a viselike control over the Soviet Union and its satellite states, and his attitude towards perceived enemies of the Soviet Union was one of unbending suspicion and hostility. His actions were driven by a paranoid fear of those who might seek to challenge his supreme authority, either from within the Communist Party or beyond Soviet borders.

More than any other individual, Stalin had been responsible for destroying the dream of collective responsibility between East and West originally held by Roosevelt and Churchill. The West had played its part in the deterioration of East-West relations, but it had essentially reacted to moves initiated by the East. Now that Stalin was gone, perhaps his successors could preside over a thaw in the Cold War.

▼ Stalinism at its worst. The remains of some 15,000 Poles slaughtered by the Soviet secret police (NKVD) following the partition of Poland between Germany and the Soviet Union in September 1939.

POST-KOREA

The end of the Korean War brought home some important lessons for both East and West. The United States noted the Soviet Union's reluctance to commit its forces openly outside the Eastern bloc, while the Soviets realized that the United States was prepared to use armed force, and perhaps even nuclear weapons, to resist communist expansion.

The Korean War had also shown both sides that, through sheer numbers, the less sophisticated military power of China and the Soviet Union could match the United States' superior technology. This knowledge increased the possibility that the United States might resort to nuclear weapons in the case of an all-out war. By the end of 1953, however, both the United States and the Soviet Union had developed the hydrogen bomb, which was considerably more powerful than the atomic bomb. A balance of terror had now been established that only a madman would dare upset.

▲ Communist Viet Minh troops gather for an attack on the French forces occupying Vietnam in January 1951. France's subsequent defeat and withdrawal led to active U.S. military involvement in the region.

A LITTLE WARMTH

By December 1953 other Cold War issues were also nearing resolution. The Soviet Union seemed reconciled to losing influence in Austria, which had been partitioned since 1945. The anti-imperialist forces in Indochina (Laos, Cambodia, and Vietnam) were on the verge of driving out U.S.-backed French troops. In the United States, Senator Joseph McCarthy's fanatical communist witch-hunt was finally running out of steam. The American people, it seemed, were beginning to realize that there was not a Red under every bed.

"AN INESTIMABLE LOSS"

On hearing of Stalin's death, Mao Tse-Tung sent an open telegram to the Soviet Union in the *Beijing People's Daily* newspaper on March 7, 1953, expressing his condolences. Behind the sorrow, however, probably lay some relief at the passing of so difficult an ally.

"It was with boundless grief that the Chinese people, the Chinese government, and I myself learned the news of the passing away of the Chinese people's closest friend and great teacher, Comrade Stalin. This is an inestimable loss, not only for the people of the Soviet Union, but for the Chinese people, for the entire camp of peace and democracy, and for peace-loving people throughout the world."

The Red Scare. Wisconsin senator Joseph McCarthy, leader of the anti-communist witch-hunt of the early 1950s, shows some of his "evidence" to the press.

ENEMIES WITHIN

Only a nation so anxious about the communist threat could have taken seriously Senator Joseph McCarthy's vague, almost hysterical accusations, such as the ones he made in a speech to the Women's Club of Wheeling, West Virginia, in February 1950:

"When a great democracy is destroyed it will not be because of the enemies from outside, but rather because of enemies within. At the end of the war we were the strongest nation on earth and morally the most powerful. Yet ... we have failed miserably ... because of ... traitors. ... In my opinion the State Department ... is thoroughly infested with communists."

THE ARMS RACE

The Cold War ended with the collapse of communism in Eastern Europe in 1989 and 1990. Until then, the features of the Cold War that were in place by 1953 remained largely intact. One such feature was a crippling arms race, as each side sought to keep up with the other.

In 1948, U.S. expenditures on defense totalled about $11 billion. By 1951 the amount had risen to nearly $35 billion and two years later it had soared to over $50 billion. During the same period, Soviet expenditures climbed from around $13 billion to $25 billion.

OTHER CONSEQUENCES

Another feature of the Cold War was the increased hostility among the American people towards communism in general and the Soviet Union in particular. Soviet citizens had long been accustomed to propaganda attacks on enemies of the state, whether foreign powers or supposed subversives within, but in peacetime America such antagonism had been relatively uncommon. Now, however, the books of left-leaning writers were shunned by schools and libraries, while anti-communist works, such as the British writer George Orwell's *Animal Farm* (1945), were embraced. Even Hollywood joined the anti-Soviet bandwagon with films like *My Son John* (1952).

The most chilling example of anti-communist hysteria in the United States was the communist witch-hunt led by

Senator Joseph McCarthy between 1950 and 1953. In February 1950, McCarthy claimed he had evidence of fifty-seven active communists working within the U.S. State Department, which was responsible for foreign affairs. In a series of hearings before the Senate Sub-committee on Investigations, some of which were televised, McCarthy's bullying and inflammatory questioning ruined the lives of many innocent people. In 1954 he was censured by the Senate for his actions.

Waging war from a distance also became a familiar feature of the Cold War. The Soviets' tactics in Korea — supplying arms and advisers but not committing its own men to the front line — were later adopted by Eastern and Western countries alike for several conflicts, notably the Arab-Israeli wars.

SPIES AND NONALIGNMENT

As each side tried to discover the other's military plans and secrets, spying also became an enduring aspect of the Cold War, as did the the emergence of nonaligned nations, most notably India, that refused to take sides in the East-West rivalry. Finally, the use of UN forces in the Korean War (page 48) guaranteed that U.S.-Soviet hostility would prevent the United Nations from fulfilling its role as an active peacekeeper.

▶ Weapons of a Soviet assassin-spy handed over to U.S. authorities in 1954: two poison-bullet guns hidden in cigarette cases (top) and a three-barreled electric gun (right) that fired poison dum-dum bullets.

THE DANGEROUS PHASE

Between 1946 and 1953, the Cold War was in its most dangerous phase. This period began with a postwar world that was devastated and disoriented. Wartime alliances were blown away by an aggressive jockeying for position in a new political environment that offered few certainties. For instance, there was no guarantee that the United States would not withdraw into isolation, as it had done after World War I.

Gradually, order emerged out of the chaos. This order, however, was unlike any the world had seen before. It featured two superpowers wedded to opposing ideologies, armed to the teeth, terrified of each other's ambitions and determined not to lose strategic advantage. It was a situation ripe for war.

AVOIDING THE BOMB

Yet no major wars came. Ironically, war was avoided for the same reason the period was so terrifying — nuclear weapons became a reality. Until August 1949, the Soviets knew that all-out war would probably mean the destruction of much of

▼ The city of Hiroshima six months after its destruction by an atomic bomb in 1945. A fear on both sides of repeating such horrific destruction produced a "balance of terror" that often prevented the Cold War from escalating out of control.

the Soviet Union. After 1949 the Soviets also possessed nuclear weapons, and the horrific possibility of a nuclear holocaust hung over the East-West rivalry. Since each side knew that the other side would probably use nuclear weapons as a very last resort, each side tried not to force the other side into a corner from which nuclear attack was the only exit.

For all their aggressive posturing and hostile rhetoric, the strategies of both the United States and the Soviet Union were largely defensive. The United States sought to contain communism, while the Soviet Union sought to protect both its borders and its way of life. Stalin's aggression in Eastern Europe, Berlin, and Korea was intended either to boost his security or to test U.S. resolve.

The two superpowers played a highly dangerous game, however, one that might easily have gone wrong. Credit should be given to individual players — such as Truman, Eisenhower, and even Stalin — for sticking to the rules of the game. If a leader with a different mentality headed either superpower, the Cold War might well have had more disastrous consequences.

▲ Nikita Khrushchev, the Soviet premier who spoke of "peaceful coexistence" between East and West. He may have saved the world from nuclear destruction by backing down during the Cuban Missile Crisis of 1962.

AN UNCERTAIN OUTLOOK

By the fall of 1953, tensions between East and West remained as broad as ever, but they had been clarified, institutionalized, stabilized. In time, the new Soviet premier, Nikita Khrushchev, would talk of the East and West living in "peaceful coexistence." If coexistence seemed a possibility, however, no one was sure if the balance of terror would keep it peaceful.

"PEACEFUL COEXISTENCE"

At a summit conference with President Eisenhower in May 1960, the Soviet premier Nikita Khrushchev took a hostile stance against the United States for spying on the Soviet Union. Yet he still held out the prospect of peaceful coexistence in the future.

"The Soviet government is profoundly convinced that if not this U.S. government, then another, and if not another, then a third, will understand that there is no other solution than peaceful coexistence of the two systems, ... capitalist and ... socialist. It is either peaceful coexistence, or war, which would spell disaster ..."

Time Line

1937

JULY Japan invades eastern China

1939

AUGUST Nazis and Soviets sign Non-aggression Pact

SEPTEMBER World War II breaks out in Europe

1941

JUNE Nazis attack Soviet Union; Atlantic Charter is signed

DECEMBER Japanese attack Pearl Harbor, United States enters war

1945

FEBRUARY Yalta Conference held

APRIL Roosevelt dies, Truman becomes U.S. president

MAY World War II ends in Europe

JUNE UN Charter established

JULY Potsdam Conference held

AUGUST Atomic bombs dropped on Hiroshima and Nagasaki; Japan surrenders

1948

FEBRUARY Communists take over in Czechoslovakia

JUNE Soviets blockade Berlin (to May 1949)

1949

APRIL NATO founded

AUGUST Soviets successfully test their first nuclear device

OCTOBER Communist People's Republic of China established

1951

APRIL Truman dismisses General MacArthur as commander of U.S. forces in Korea

1943

NOVEMBER Tehran Conference is held by "Big Three"

1946

Civil war begins in China (to 1949)

1947

MARCH Truman unveils Truman Doctrine to Congress

JUNE Marshall Plan for Western Europe is announced

JULY CIA established

AUGUST India gains independence

SEPTEMBER Cominform created

DECEMBER Civil war breaks out in Vietnam (to 1954)

1950

JANUARY United States authorizes deployment of hydrogen bomb

FEBRUARY Senator McCarthy begins communist witch-hunt (to 1953)

FEBRUARY China and Soviet Union sign Treaty of Friendship, Alliance, and Mutual Assistance

JUNE Korean War begins

OCTOBER China enters Korean War

1952

NOVEMBER Eisenhower elected U.S. president

1953

MARCH Stalin dies

JULY Korean War ends

1991

Soviet Union breaks up

Glossary

appease: to make concessions to a person or country so as to avoid conflict.

arms race: escalating military buildup of the United States and the Soviet Union during the Cold War.

atomic bomb: earliest form of nuclear weapon, based on nuclear fission.

Big Three: World War II Allied leaders Roosevelt (United States), Churchill (Britain), and Stalin (Soviet Union).

bloc: group of countries.

capitalism: economic system in which an open competitive market determines all prices and wages.

CIA: acronym for Central Intelligence Agency, established in 1947 to manage U.S. foreign intelligence operations.

coalition: political or military partnership.

Cominform: Communist Information Bureau, which coordinated activities of European communist parties.

communism: ideology that advocates government ownership of property and often results in authoritarian rule.

containment: U.S. policy meant to prevent the spread of communism.

conventional weapons: traditional, or nonnuclear, weapons.

embargo: blockade or ban on trade.

hydrogen bomb: later nuclear weapon, based on nuclear fusion.

ideology: belief or way of thinking, as in communist or free-market ideology.

imperialism: expansion of a nation's empire through occupation or control of other territories or countries.

Iron Curtain: border between Eastern and Western Europe during the Cold War.

lend-lease: U.S. system for granting aid to U.S. allies during World War II.

liberal democracy: ideology that advocates an elected, representative government that has loose control over a capitalist economy.

Marshall Plan: program that provided massive aid from the United States to Western European countries to help them rebuild after World War II.

NATO: acronym for North Atlantic Treaty Organization, a defensive alliance of Western nations established in 1949.

non-aggression pact: agreement between nations not to fight each other

propaganda: information, whether true or false, that is spread with the aim of helping or hurting a particular cause, group of people, or government.

purge: to eliminate individuals from an organization, usually by force.

reparations: after war, goods or money collected by a victorious country from a defeated country for damages inflicted during wartime.

secretary of state: U.S. official responsible, under the president, for conducting U.S. foreign policy.

Security Council: decision-making body of the United Nations.

Truman Doctrine: U.S. policy, first outlined by President Truman, that sought to defend any peoples whose freedom was threatened.

United Nations: organization of nations first established in 1945 to safeguard world peace and foster international cooperation.

Books

Cold War: An Illustrated History, 1945–1991
Jeremy Isaacs and Taylor Downing
(Oxford University Press)

The Cold War (*Guides to Historic Events
of the Twentieth Century* series)
Katherine A. S. Sibley (Greenwood Press)

The Origins of the Cold War: 1941–1949
Martin McCauley (Addison-Wesley)

Russia, America and the Cold War: 1949–1991
(*Seminar Studies in History* series)
Martin McCauley (Longman)

Videos

Birth of a Cold War (*NBC White Papers*)
(New Video Group)

Brave New World: The Cold War Begins
(WGBH Boston Video)

CNN Perspectives Presents: The Cold War
(Turner Home Video)

The Korean War: Fire and Ice
(A & E Entertainment)

*Time Machine — Berlin Airlift:
The First Battle of the Cold War*
(A & E Home Video)

Web Sites

Cold War International History Project
cwihp.si.edu/default.htm

The Cold War Museum
www.coldwar.org

The Harvard Project on Cold War Studies
www.fas.harvard.edu/~hpcws/

Index